HMRC – Her Majesty's Roller Coaster

BDO LLP is the world's fifth largest professional services firm and accounting network, providing audit, tax and advisory services to start-ups, SMEs, AIM-listed, FTSE 100 and multi-national clients. In the UK, we are recognised as leaders in exceptional client service, with 3,500 staff in 22 offices and over 300 partners. Globally, we operate in 144 countries, with over 55,000 people working out of 1,250 offices.

Daniel Dover is a senior partner at BDO LLP, and a recognised specialist in tax disputes and disclosures. His expertise covers all UK HMRC Specialist Investigation office matters, including those involving questions of domicile and residence of both corporate and private entities. Daniel is also involved in advising businesses and families with their strategic direction and future. He is a trustee of a number of prominent charities and advises a wide range of charities on the tax pitfalls and governance issues they face. He is the co-author of *The Taxman Always Rings Twice*, *An Inspector Returns*, *War and Peace* and *An Inspector Calls*.

12

Tim Hindle is the author of sev~ ~ss and finance, including *~ Sultan of Berkeley Square*, ~man-agement editor a ~und-ing editor of *EuroB* ~d he has written many b ~kish li ~m.

520 799 08 8

Her Majesty's Roller Coaster

Hints on how to survive a tax investigation

Daniel Dover
and
Tim Hindle

with cartoons by
Pugh

P

PROFILE BOOKS

First published in Great Britain in 2014 by
PROFILE BOOKS LTD
3A Exmouth House
Pine Street
Exmouth Market
London ECIR OJH
www.profilebooks.com

Copyright © BDO 2014
55 Baker Street
London WIU 7EU
www.bdo.co.uk

The moral right of the authors has been asserted.

Cartoons by Pugh, courtesy of the *Daily Mail*.

All rights reserved. Without limiting the rights under copyright reserved
above, no part of this publication may be reproduced, stored or introduced
into a retrieval system, or transmitted, in any form or by any means
(electronic, mechanical, photocopying, recording or otherwise), without the
prior written permission of both the copyright owner and the publisher of
this book.

A CIP catalogue record for this book is available from the British Library.

ISBN 978 1 78125 315 1
eISBN 978 1 78283 093 1

Typeset in Columbus by MacGuru Ltd
info@macguru.org.uk
Printed in Great Britain by
Bell & Bain Ltd

While care has been taken to ensure the accuracy of the contents of this
book, it is intended to provide general guidance only and does not
constitute professional advice. The information contained in this book is
based on the authors' understanding of legislation, regulation and practice at
the time of publication, all of which is subject to change, possibly with
retrospective effect. Neither they nor BDO LLP can therefore accept any
legal or regulatory liability from readers acting on the information given.

Contents

Acknowledgements

We are truly grateful to many people for their help in the production of this book.

In particular, we thank Fiona Fernie for her considerable contribution and involvement in this project, together of course with 'the Team'.

Special thanks are also due to Holly Raymen of BDO for her sterling work on the front line. She kept as cool a head when fearlessly testing rides at theme parks all over the land as when bringing the participants in this venture into line and keeping us on time and on track.

Stuart Gerber, Richard Morley and Dawn Register were unstinting in their encouragement and support.

Thanks too are due to Pugh, who captured all the twists, turns and bumps of the ride with his cartoons.

We also thank our long-suffering wives Helen and Ellian. They watched us jump on and off many a ride, but their support each time never wavers. They ensured we were never derailed.

Lastly, our thanks to Andrew Franklin and the team

at Profile Books, without whom (of course) this would never have happened. So blame them! Or alternatively you can blame HMRC – nothing could have happened without them either… so we also owe them our heartfelt thanks!

Daniel I. Dover
Tim Hindle
September 2014

Foreword

Most people are happy to pay their dues to the taxman. But no one wants to pay more than they have to. Much of the debate about tax today revolves around the words 'have to'. How much do we have to pay? And how much do we not have to pay?

The answer is not straightforward. On the whole, taxpayers want a clear set of rules by which they can calculate their true obligations to the state. Yet, despite reams of legislation aimed at helping them to have a more transparent view of how much tax they are expected to pay, the picture only seems to get murkier as the years go by. More and more people feel compelled to seek specialist outside advice about their tax affairs. It is so easy to get the sums wrong.

This book gives the reader a small taste of the issues that might arise should Her Majesty's Revenue & Customs (HMRC) decide that, in a particular individual's case, the sums are indeed wrong and insufficient tax has been paid. It combines and updates BDO's previous books in the series – *An Inspector Returns, War or Peace* and *The Taxman Always Rings Twice*, all of them already classics of their genre.

It also comes with a health warning. Whatever you do, don't get into a serious skirmish with HMRC without decent intelligence, far more of it than can be provided in this slim volume.

Introduction

In recent years, tax evasion has become a hot political issue. George Osborne, while chancellor of the exchequer, said that tax evasion is 'morally repugnant…it's stealing from law-abiding people who face higher taxes in order to make good the lost revenue.' Part of the problem is that the meaning of 'tax evasion' shifts to suit the speaker's purpose.

The UK government's primary focus has been on corporate tax. A number of high-profile cases involving companies like Apple, Google and Starbucks have suggested that multinationals can effectively make themselves stateless for tax purposes. One commentator was moved to say that corporation tax is now 'as voluntary as a collection plate passed around at the end of a church service'. Corporation tax accounts for only 7 per cent of all UK tax receipts.

Despite the world's many other problems, Britain chose to put the issue at the top of its agenda for a meeting of the G8 group of rich countries which it hosted in June 2013. The outcome of the meeting – a pledge to stop companies shifting profits to low-cost tax havens – had, said the prime minister David Cameron, 'the potential to rewrite the rules on tax'.

A few months later, at a meeting in Russia, the larger G20 group of nations made a similar pledge. The G20's communique said it would be putting forward suggestions for a system whereby corporate profits would be taxed 'where economic activities deriving the profits are performed, and where value is created'.

Such things are easier said than done. Nevertheless, politicians are clearly baying for blood, despite the fact that several of them have been caught recently with their own fiscal pants down. Their failure to rein in public expenditure has sent them in search of new ways to manage their nations' unmanageable debts without, they hope, losing votes in the process. And their eyes have fallen not just on corporations that may have paid less tax than their chancellor would have liked them to. They have also fallen on individuals in a similar predicament.

Although over half of all individuals' income tax is paid by the top 10 per cent of taxpayers (and around 30 per cent by the top 1 per cent), there is a feeling that the rich are not paying their full share. The comedian Jimmy Carr was criticised by the prime minister in 2012 for using a controversial Jersey-based offshore tax scheme. Carr admitted at the time that he had made a 'terrible error of judgement', had left the scheme, and

would subsequently conduct his financial affairs 'more responsibly'. Nevertheless, a year later he was booed off the stage at the Hackney Empire in east London by hecklers shouting, 'Pay your taxes!'

The UK government continued to pile on the fiscal pressure. Its 2014 budget contained proposals to allow HMRC to take unpaid tax directly from a taxpayer's bank account. (Previously the Revenue could only do this with the permission of a court.) A powerful committee of MPs deemed the plan to be 'very concerning'. The committee was also concerned about a proposal to compel upfront payments of tax in disputed cases related to special avoidance schemes.

Then, a mere month after his budget, George Osborne made it clear that this was not to be enough. 'We are changing the balance of the law,' he announced, 'so that the burden of proof falls on those who are hiding their money offshore.' By this he meant that the government intends (after consultation) to make it a criminal offence for anyone to have an offshore income and not to declare it. It will then no longer be necessary for HMRC to prove that there was an intention to evade paying tax before sending a taxpayer off to jail. Genuine mistakes and misunderstandings will no longer be automatic 'Get Out of Jail Free' cards.

At the same time, the government announced its intention to look at ways to increase the penalties for non-payment of tax – at present, fines can amount to twice the unpaid tax that is due. Meanwhile a network of agreements between different tax authorities comes into force in 2016. These allow for the automatic exchange of information about UK residents' bank accounts in offshore centres. The chancellor says that for 'those who are hiding their money offshore', there is now 'no safe haven and we will find you'. Somalia, of course, remains an option.

One of the consequences of this tax hunt is that Her Majesty's Revenue & Customs, the nation's tax collector, is under new pressure to catch those deemed to have paid too little tax, both companies and individuals. A

powerful committee of MPs went so far as to accuse HMRC of losing its nerve 'when it comes to mounting prosecutions against multinational corporations'.

For this, and for other reasons (HMRC's access to a whole new range of information, for example), a growing number of people are receiving what are known as 'Mae West' letters. These are sent by the taxman (see page 17) and suggest that he or she (an increasing number of them are women) might want you, the taxpayer, to 'come up and see me sometime', in the famous phrase of the once-famous blonde. At the end of 2011 over 6,000 people in the UK received just such a letter. HMRC had discovered that they had (not all of them legally) been enjoying the benefits of a Swiss bank account.

The emphasis of the Revenue's letters, however, has been shifting in recent years. Now HMRC's attitude has a more menacing undertone: 'Come up and see me sometime,' it seems to say, 'and make it snappy. Before I come up and see you.'

Fasten your belts

Anyone whose financial affairs come under the scrutiny of an HMRC inspector is in for an emotional roller-coaster ride. In the first few moments of realisation – usually after opening an ominous brown envelope with the letters 'HMRC' on its cover – terror and denial are common reactions, followed in quick succession by anger and regret.

From that moment on, the taxpayer's life can feel a bit like a visit to one of Britain's great theme parks – places full of roller-coaster rides and scary experiences that no one chooses to visit on their own. Who wants to sit in the Titanic Typhoon or the Crash Pad without a comforter at their side, someone they can scream along with at the most scary moments?

It helps too to have a comforter by your side during a tax investigation, someone who knows from experience how such journeys tend to unfold and who understands

A Code of Practice 9 letter from HMRC

Dear xxxx

HMRC has information that gives it reason to suspect that you have committed tax fraud. I intend to investigate the suspected tax fraud so am notifying you that HMRC's Investigation of Fraud Code of Practice 9 (COP9) applies to your tax affairs from the issue date of this letter. My investigation will cover all of your tax affairs.

The Code of Practice 9 enclosed governs how HMRC investigates suspected fraud. You should read the Code of Practice carefully as you need to decide if you wish to co-operate with my investigation. I will ask you to confirm you have read and understood the COP9 before I can engage with you or any representatives you instruct…

…HMRC recommends that you discuss this letter with an adviser who has knowledge and experience of our COP9 investigation of fraud procedures.

Yours sincerely

Investigator

the taxman's jargon, for there is plenty of that. There are also plenty of enigmatic signs about future progress displayed discreetly along the way, some of which have been known to elicit earth-shattering screams from those who have spotted them.

Taxpayers should never be lulled into thinking that an investigation will be like a stroll around the old Crystal Palace, sometimes described as 'the world's first theme park'. Theme-park rides and tax inspectors have moved with the times. Both have been upgraded in recent years – with new loops, new skills and new challenges.

Once upon a time, inspectors used to write polite letters from musty offices after finishing the day's *Times* crossword. Now they are more likely to pay an unannounced visit on their way home from a martial-arts class and throw taxpayers into a spin such as they won't experience this side of the legendary Smiler at Alton Towers.

There are a number of other features that a tax investigation has in common with a day out at a theme park:

1. **Feelings of disorientation**. It is easy to lose one's sense of direction on Her Majesty's Roller Coaster, as on any other. Everything is not always as it seems. The overhanging branch is a sleeping creature; the clause allowing capital gains to be offset against losses applies only to a group of people to whom you do not, you belatedly discover, belong.

2. **Regular stomach churnings**. This is of course the central experience of most theme parks as they try to build ever more death-defying rides. It is also a central experience in any investigation of an individual's tax affairs. As the taxman takes his time to come to the all-important decision on your fiscal fate, and as your hopes of redemption slowly crumble, you can only wonder at how indigestion can be so severe when not a morsel has passed your lips.

3. **Hidden obstacles galore**. At the beginning it is tempting to think that your case is so strong that it will be impossible for the taxman not to give you an early and generous reprieve. But don't be fooled. Once you have received the HMRC letter, your course is unlikely to be smooth. Hidden obstacles may start to appear – a CCTV photo proving that you were in Geneva when you claim you were visiting your sick mother in her Scarborough nursing home; a former wife who turns out to have a photographic memory of all your offshore bits and pieces, and an archive of historic material in support.

4. **Heroes and villains**. Theme parks are full of heroes and villains. There is Superman and Cinderella; and there is Captain Hook and Cruella de Ville. Heroes and villains appear frequently too in the stories of tax investigations. And whilst it is

Discovery Arcade: From start to finish

A typical journey through one of the taxman's favourite amusements

Notification letter from HMRC or voluntary disclosure

An investigation is prompted either when HMRC believes it has a case to pursue or if you, the taxpayer, volunteer information to the Revenue.

Appointment of advisers

As soon as you are aware that an investigation is under way, appoint a team of professional advisers before you do anything else.

Initial meeting with HMRC

Your advisers will then meet HMRC to assess the seriousness of the case. At this stage it is not necessary for you to attend. In fact, it's better if you don't.

COP8 or COP9 investigation

You will then be told which type of investigation your case comes under. The most usual are Code of Practice 9 or CDF, Contractual Disclosure Facility, which usually means you are under investigation for fraud, and Code of Practice 8, which covers other forms of non-payment.
(See pages 64–5 for further details.)

Scoping meeting

Your advisers will usually meet the CDF team to discuss the scope of the investigation. This is commonly known as a 'scoping meeting'.

Clarification meeting

Later the investigators may meet your advisers again to discuss outstanding queries. This usually marks the beginning of the negotiation of a settlement.

Settlement meeting

This marks the end of the negotiation. HMRC invites you to propose a settlement, which is usually a formality unless there are still issues to be resolved.

Letter of offer

This is a formal letter to HMRC, drawn up by your advisers and signed by you.

Formal acceptance

HMRC replies in due course, confirming its acceptance of your offer.

The ultimate goal at the end of the Discovery Arcade is to emerge without serious damage – i.e., to reach a settlement without any criminal investigation. The settlement is a contractual agreement involving a letter with a written offer, to which there has to be a written acceptance. It necessarily involves compromise, which leaves both sides less than perfectly content. Rich and powerful taxpayers who have not been used to making concessions during their lives can find this process difficult. But, if their advisers have served them well, they will end up feeling less unhappy about the settlement than HMRC.

easy to assume that the taxpayer is always the hero and the tax inspector the villain, that is not always the case. Ever more frequently, criminals are jailed not for the drug dealing, sex crimes or financial scams that the law tries to nail them for, but for the tax that they have never paid. After more than 50 trials that failed to find him guilty, the billionaire former prime minister of Italy, Silvio Berlusconi, was finally sentenced to four years in prison in October 2012 for buying TV rights at artificially inflated prices in order to avoid paying taxes. At his appeal he was described as the 'author of a whole system of tax fraud'.

There is one notable distinction between a visit to the likes of Chessington and time spent on the taxman's roller coaster. Whereas a visit to Chessington rarely lasts longer than a day, a visit to the taxman's lair is never going to be over in such a short period of time.

As the investigation of your tax affairs continues, you can find yourself emotionally bruised by the taxman's methods. Up in the air one minute with relief that the VAT vampires have left, down in the doldrums the next at the prospect of spending time in HMRC's dungeons, it's not totally unlike a day at one of the many theme parks in this still great and heavily-taxed land of ours.

This book is designed to help taxpayers emerge from

the experience in one piece and with as many of their assets intact as is appropriate. The advice of any experienced professional is: don't panic, and get expert help at the outset – before you enter the park and before you get taken on any of its rides. At the very least you'll need someone to help you with the jargon. Only then can you head safely for Rumba Rapids, the Swarm or Hocus Pocus Hall with the hope that you will survive the thrill and continue with your life thereafter.

1

Avoision

'The Twister'

Once upon a time there was something called tax avoidance, and there was something called tax evasion, and everyone knew that one was legal and the other was not. It was as clear as the distinction between a zoo and a theme park. But recently the meaning of these words has become twisted. Now there is Chessington World of Adventures, which is both a zoo and a theme park, and there is a thing called 'avoision', a word invented in 1979 by an English economist, Arthur Seldon, to describe what has been defined as 'the grey area of ambiguous acts that fall between legal avoidance and illegal evasion of the law's prescriptions'.

Research by the Tax Justice Network, an organisation that opposes 'loopholes and distortions in tax and regulation, and the abuses that flow from them', suggests that tax evasion costs the UK in the region of £70 billion a year, an amount that is more than half the country's total annual health-care bill. The number is debatable

but, suffice it to say, there is a form of hard-core tax evasion which remains substantial and indisputable – for example, where some sort of dishonesty is involved, especially the non-disclosure of relevant facts or the creation of fake documents. Around that hard core, however, there is now a vast penumbra of uncertainty where it is not possible any longer to distinguish clearly between avoidance and evasion.

The French have decided to muddy the waters (not for the first time, as far as the English are concerned) by choosing to use the expression '*evasion fiscal*' when they mean 'tax avoidance'. This provides ample opportunity for misunderstanding in the international forums that are increasingly influential in framing tax legislation. It is as if *nos chers voisins* had chosen to call Paris's Disneyland, Le Disney World, just to confuse it with the rather more exciting destination with almost the same name located in Orlando, Florida.

The General Anti-Abuse Rule (GAAR), a piece of legislation that came into effect in July 2013, is one part of the UK government's more forceful approach to perceived 'tax dodgers'. It was introduced to help HMRC tackle what it defines as 'abusive avoidance'. This is avoidance that falls short of blatant evasion but has, nevertheless, a similar motive. Although such a scheme has worked well in Canada, it is still uncharted territory for the UK and is yet to be tested in the courts. At least one eminent QC has expressed a low opinion of the GAAR. 'Bad law drives out good law,' says David Goldberg QC. And 'this GAAR will be bad law'.

Governments are rarely single-minded about avoision. On the one hand they trumpet the need to take action on tax dodgers, whilst on the other creating things like tax-free savings certificates under the National Savings & Investments (NS&I) scheme, a scheme which

encourages 'tax mitigation'. In truth, 'tax mitigation' is little more than a polite way of saying 'tax avoidance'.

The area is more vexed for companies than it is for individuals. They are under an obligation to shareholders to keep their costs down and their profits up. So their motive for seeking ways to lower their tax bill is rather different. However, a number of landmark cases from way back in 1982 (known as the Ramsay cases) have clarified that any scheme which lacks 'a business purpose' other than to save tax will be struck down and the tax bill calculated as if it were not in place. In 2013 a

Supreme Court judge, Lord Walker, said that since the Ramsay cases 'there has been an increasingly strong and general recognition that artificial tax avoidance is a social evil which puts an unfair burden on the shoulders of those who do not adopt such measures.'

Nevertheless, there is no shortage of people eager to advise taxpayers on ways in which they can reduce the amount of tax that they pay. Some of the ways they recommend are perfectly legal; but some of them are not. America's Internal Revenue Service (IRS) says that 'taxpayers need to remember that if it sounds too good to be true, it probably is.'

2

Onshore and offshore

The Tidal Wave

Remember those pretty offshore places where secrecy ensured that your private affairs remained just that – private? Places like Switzerland, Monte Carlo and the Bahamas, described by one British taxpayer who chose to live there in fiscal exile as 'the original sunny place for shady people'? Well, life is becoming increasingly difficult for tax havens like these. A spate of information-sharing agreements between countries has meant that fewer and fewer of them can remain tax 'heavens'.

What's more, many such places have become about as leaky as a holed water slide. Information has at times flowed out of them like a tidal wave – some of it from whistleblowers (see page 47) who find it easier to nick a computer stick than to walk off with piles of paper; some of it from new cross-border treaties on the exchange of

information. The Tidal Wave ride at Surrey's Thorpe Park is described as 'a super soaking tsunami of thrills'. Where secret bank accounts are concerned you can forget the thrills. The tidal wave of data flowing out of leaky offshore centres these days can drown you thrill-lessly in less time than it takes to say 'Gotcha'.

In practice, the really heavy hitters in the tax-haven world are much closer to home, in places like Ireland and the Netherlands, the state of Delaware, and our own dear UK. Early in 2013, Google was criticised by UK MPs for channelling £3.2 billion of its UK sales through Dublin and paying little tax in the process. At about the same time, the chief executive of the Apple computer business was questioned by US lawmakers about the billions of dollars that it then retained in its Irish divisions, while the American coffee chain Starbucks was quizzed about royalty payments that it transfers to a Dutch sister company. The multinationals themselves claim that the schemes they use are all legal.

'The world is flat', wrote Thomas Friedman in a book of the same title about the phenomenon of globalisation making things the same the world over. One thing he was definitely not referring to was different countries' rates of tax. They still vary greatly across the globe. France and the Netherlands, separated only by tiny Belgium, have regimes about as different as Coney Island and Thorpe Park. Companies that are genuinely global are, within limits, free to pick and choose the rates they pay.

But they walk a fine line between the gains they make from paying lower rates of tax and the losses that increasingly accrue from boycotts by consumers who feel that companies' low tax bills are not fair. Consumers do react, albeit briefly, to news about, for example, how Amazon received more in grants from the Scottish government in 2012 than it paid in UK tax. Or how Starbucks voluntarily agreed to hand over £20 million to the British taxman after an outcry about the fact that it had

not paid a penny to HMRC for three years in a row. 'Time', said prime minister David Cameron with an eye on the ballot box and a neat turn of phrase, 'for businesses to wake up and smell the coffee.'

3

Non-doms

Aliens from outer spaces

One of the most controversial aspects of British tax law, and one that lies at the heart of claims that the country is an exceptionally advantageous tax haven for the super-rich, is the treatment of people who are known as 'non-doms'. Non-doms are UK residents for tax purposes, but they were (usually) not born in the UK and they state that they do not intend to die there. Of course, however much in control of their lives they might think they are, death can still take them by surprise. So the key question is not so much where they want to die as where they want to be buried.

Non-doms are a sort of exotic bird of passage, and they include Russian oligarchs and Arab sheikhs living not a muezzin's call away from Marble Arch. There have been a small number of cases where the children of non-domiciled parents have established non-domiciled status for themselves even though they were born in the UK and spent much of their lives in the country. But the vast majority of non-doms originally came from somewhere else.

For such people there is a special set of tax rules, rules that are less onerous than those for common-or-garden Brits who were born somewhere between Land's End and John O'Groats. The treatment they receive differs according to the tax in question. As far as inheritance tax is concerned, non-doms are deemed to be domiciled in the UK once they have been resident here for 17 out of the previous 20 years. But for the purposes of income tax and capital-gains tax they can remain non-domiciled for the whole of their lives – unless, that is, they are female and they married a UK-domiciled person before 1974.

Non-doms can in certain circumstances keep income from abroad in offshore accounts free of tax for as long as they do not remit that income to the UK. Until recently, the income that non-doms received overseas was taxed in the UK only to the extent that it was remitted back to the country. However, since the 2008/09 tax year, non-doms who have been in the UK for seven years or more can opt for this so-called 'remittance basis' of taxation only if they pay an annual lump sum to HMRC. For those who have been in the UK for more than 12 years, the sum is currently £50,000.

For some this is still less onerous than it would be in other countries – in nearby France, for instance, where the top rate of income tax is currently 45 per cent, or in

the United States where all US passport-holders are taxed on their worldwide income and capital gains, regardless of where it arises or (indeed) of where they want to be buried.

Because of their status, non-doms have some distinctive behaviour patterns. For one thing, they do an unusually large amount of shopping outside the UK. So they tend to prefer Disneyland near Paris, or Coney Island outside New York, to the UK's own home-grown theme parks. That way they can pay for their rides with money that stays legitimately outside the UK's tax net. Not only do they then avoid paying direct taxes into Britain's coffers, they also avoid paying UK indirect taxes, taxes such as the dreaded Value Added Tax (VAT).

UK governments have moments when they would love to get rid of non-doms. But they invariably hesitate to abolish their special status when they contemplate the loss to the country that could follow should this crowd of predominantly wealthy folk take their homes and their investments elsewhere. Governments could be said to want to be on the roundabouts and the swings at the same time – or, in other words, to be able to eat their candy-floss and to keep it. Tricky one…

The big sleep-over

Residence is a different concept from domicile. But it too is important for tax purposes. A person's residence is determined by the number of days that he or she spends in the country. Before April 2013 it was quite simple: if a person slept in the UK for fewer than 90 nights in any one year then he or she was deemed to be non-resident. There were special rules for people like airline pilots and cabin crew, people who spent much of their time working in the air, in a space that has not (yet) been claimed by any tax authority. Since April 2013, however, the rules have become much more complicated so that now even cabin crew need tax advisers. It is possible for someone to be deemed resident when they have spent as few as 16 nights of the year in the country.

In days gone by, British taxpayers who were unhappy with income-tax rates at home would move to places like Malta or Monaco for the 276 days or so every year that they needed to spend abroad in order to establish non-residence in the UK. Now they are as likely to be holed up in a beach bungalow on Thailand's Andaman coast or at a faraway condo in Phoenix, Arizona. And they can do little more than take their summer holidays in the UK.

In an age when the passports of travellers passing from one European Union (EU) country to another are rarely stamped, it is not as easy as it once was for HMRC to demonstrate that taxpayers have failed to observe the non-residence rules. Nevertheless, travellers' movements are not entirely opaque. Don't, for instance, be convinced by people who argue that the way for non-residents ('dodge 'ems') to return from Disneyland, Paris, is on the Eurostar train (inside it, not underneath it) on the grounds that passports are never stamped on that particular cross-Channel trip. That may be true. But HMRC can still gain access to Eurostar's official passenger lists to find out who came to the UK, and when.

They have other sources of help too. The names of all passengers travelling through UK airports are preserved for years. And credit-card and mobile-phone bills invariably tell tales of their own. Sailors who spend long periods of time abroad often stock up with wads of cash before they return home. That way they can avoid leaving the usual credit-card trail of the time that they have spent in the UK's pleasure spots.

4

HMRC

The Smiler

The Smiler, Alton Towers' latest and most scary ride, promises to 'marmalise your mind and body' as it takes you through a world-record 14 hoops. Taxpayers who choose to stay away from Britain's most popular theme park can nevertheless find themselves being taken through at least as many hoops by HMRC, should they be subjected to an investigation. Marmalising is for them also very much on the cards. The Smiler claims to come with special 'mind manipulations' to disorientate riders. HMRC too has a good line in mind manipulation.

There is no doubt that HMRC has toughened up over the years. As the economy's slide has become steeper, so has HMRC's slide. Inspectors are becoming more like the Customs & Excise gang, traditionally a different breed recruited separately to further Her Majesty's interests in gathering indirect taxes. The Customs & Excise gang are more like the stars of *EastEnders*, spending time in bonded warehouses and the holds of rusting

cargo ships. While there is a plan to integrate the two authorities fully, it has been moving slowly. The formal merger between them was said at the time it took place (April 2005) to be merely a first step. A second step has integrated the two organisations' penalty regimes more closely. But there is still more to come.

Tax inspectors have been forced to toughen up by adverse press criticism of the freedom that they have to negotiate so-called 'sweetheart deals' with recalcitrant taxpayers, and by changes in the rules of their game.

HMRC is no longer a preferential creditor when taxpayers or their businesses go bust. In the old days, having preference allowed inspectors to queue up in a gentlemanly manner for their share of the leftovers, knowing that they were assured of a place near the front. Now they have to make a grab for whatever they can lay their hands on, along with any other common or garden creditor.

The tax inspector's job description emphasises that HMRC is an adviser as well as a policeman. One website says that tax inspectors work 'to ensure that organisations and individuals pay the correct amount of tax at the right time. They are responsible for detecting and investigating tax evasion and, in disputed cases, will represent HMRC at independent appeal tribunals. The role also involves offering information and advice to individuals, businesses and organisations on a range of tax and related issues.'

There are certain things that tax inspectors are not. For one thing, they are not a modern-day Orwellian creation spouting 'doublethink' in attempts to trip us up. Nor are they a bunch of colourless, desk-bound apparatchiks. In 2007 a Russian tax inspector admitted that he had been recruited by MI6 to spy for Britain. And inspectors have been the subject of several dramatic works of fiction. The Australian Booker-prize-winning author Peter Carey wrote a novel called *The Tax Inspector* in which not only was the inspector a woman, but she was also unmarried… and pregnant. In Tobias Hill's *The Cryptographer*, a female tax inspector falls in love with the richest man in the world, a man she is supposed to be investigating. Unmarried mothers, Russian spies, lovers of the megarich… what next? A winner of *Britain's Got Talent*?

How many other professions have been elevated to such glamorous heights? We have not yet been offered *The Part-Time Computer Coder* or *The Offshore Commodities Trader* as a Man Booker prize contender.

Careless talk

Inspectors still have a sense of humour, but it is as well not to test it too far. They did not, for example, appreciate the joker who, when he filled in a questionnaire that asked for 'Any other income?' saw fit to answer 'F All'. He was only rescued from a fate worse than 14 successive hoops on the Smiler by explaining that he had meant it to stand for 'Family Allowance'.

For the most part, inspectors remain decent human beings who meet people in pubs and restaurants, make friends when on holiday abroad, and admire expensively renovated houses. They can be as upset by small slights as any of us. One case, which went all the way to the High Court, was started because a tax inspector was nearly mowed down by a taxpayer's Rolls-Royce emblazoned with personalised number plates.

When visiting pubs, inspectors have been known to overhear tradesmen being asked if they give discounts for cash. And they have a special sensitivity to cash. In the age of ubiquitous credit cards and online banking they find that there are fewer and fewer legitimate uses for cash in daily life.

As a means to avoid declaring income (and therefore tax), keeping cash can be risky. Not only is it highly inflammable and vulnerable to theft, but it is also prone to other less obvious dangers. One tax evader who for years

In one raid on a taxpayer's house, the investigators, the suspect, his adviser and the police were all sitting around a table when HMRC asked the taxpayer if they could see some documents. The suspect said he'd go and fetch them.

When the man had not returned after 15 minutes, the police and the investigators realised he'd done a bunk. What's more, he'd locked them all in the room. And he'd taken the documents in question along with him as he made his escape across the roof. The police missed him at Heathrow by about an hour. Needless to say, the documents all disappeared.

kept a stash in a safe-deposit box (away from the tax-man's beady eye) found that he had to swap all his notes for new ones as and when they were withdrawn from circulation. The logistics involved in taking shopping bags full of notes from a safe-deposit box to a bank in order to change them were unusually demanding. It was said to be an extreme case of 'cash and carry'.

Perhaps surprisingly, inspectors have a fondness for English literature. And the Bard comes high on their list of favourites. 'The lady doth protest too much, methinks,' is a line they are particularly fond of, since they do frequently come across a surfeit of protest – and not just from ladies. *Much Ado About Nothing* is another of their Shakespearean favourites. They so often have to put up with taxpayers suggesting that their attentions are just that.

5

Whistleblowers

Deep throats

Of all the characters in a tax investigation, whistleblowers provide the most dramatic stories. The biggest bank data leak in recent years came from a whistleblower who was a systems engineer employed at the Geneva branch of HSBC. He absconded with the names and details of some 130,000 account holders and then blew his whistle loudly in the ears of fiscal authorities around the world.

Ever since 1890, HMRC has been entitled to reward whistleblowers for their efforts. Nowadays there is a hotline for them to call and a website for them to visit. One former employee of a bank in Liechtenstein was paid £100,000 for the names of about 100 UK account holders at his bank. The employee, now in hiding, was a serial bounty hunter. He also sold information to the German authorities.

Many whistleblowers are happy to tell their tales for nothing, believing that righteous behaviour is its own reward. Few of them are aware that their life will never

be the same thereafter. When the former HSBC systems engineer was interviewed by a journalist in France in 2013, he was accompanied by three bodyguards and was wearing an artificial beard. A disturbingly high percentage of whistleblowers subsequently wilt under the pressure. They suffer from depression, turn to alcohol, and even go so far as to commit suicide.

Some whistleblowers choose to talk for less than noble reasons. For instance, people who are themselves under investigation for suspected under-payment of tax are sometimes tempted to try and do a deal. 'I'm not the only one at it,' they say. 'If I tell you about Derek and Mike down in the hall of mirrors, will you let me off?'

Those who take the least time to draw breath before

blowing a whistle are aggrieved spouses and disgruntled employees. Jealous competitors, angry neighbours and jilted lovers are also likely informers. Jilted lovers often have the attitude that if their former partner is going to live without them, then that partner is also going to live without a lot of other things besides. These may include the apartment in Marbella where the informer once spent long and happy holidays living in a style to which he or she has now had to become unaccustomed.

Former spouses can be particularly enthusiastic whistleblowers. In one case a husband claimed to HMRC that the house where he and his wife had lived was owned by an offshore company. But when the wife came to court to seek a divorce, she was able to prove that the house belonged solely to her husband – and half of it, therefore, was hers. The court's judgment – that 'by virtue of some transaction not explained … the husband was able to assemble offshore monies which later he deployed in the purchase' – would normally have been confidential. But in this case the wife's brother felt moved to bring it to the attention of HMRC.

The amounts involved in whistleblower cases can reach dizzying heights. After one individual's revelations, the US Department of Justice charged a Swiss banker with concealing from America's Internal Revenue Service (IRS) assets worth almost $20 billion in 19,000 accounts belonging to US citizens. One of those citizens turned out to be Ty Warner, billionaire inventor of the cuddly Beanie Babies doll. In 2013 he was fined over $50 million and faced a five-year jail term for forgetting to tell the IRS about his Swiss accounts.

When, in early 2012, whistleblowers at two Swiss banks handed over data about their clients' accounts to the UK tax authorities, an HMRC spokesperson at the time said: 'We get information from a wide variety of sources which we carefully examine to make sure everyone pays the right tax.' One of those sources, of course, is the taxpayer himself.

6

Voluntary disclosure

Loggers' Leap

HMRC prefers to get information direct from the horse's mouth rather than via whistleblowers, and it has always been keen to persuade its clients to tell the truth. In recent years the process of voluntary disclosure has been streamlined in an attempt to encourage more taxpayers to come clean. There are now a number of formal ways for them to reveal new information, and they became far keener to do so after several big British banks were forced to disclose the names of customers who had overseas accounts. After the disclosure, HMRC sent out more than 5,000 Mae West letters, and announced that it planned to send out yet more.

Volunteering information can help to secure a smoother ride with HMRC. But the information given should never be partial. Some people think they can get

away with disclosing only a part of the earnings that they have stashed abroad. Such people would be better off not volunteering at all. HMRC has a duty to look into everything, so it is very likely to sniff around things that have not been revealed.

And it has the nostrils of a bloodhound. One inspector looking through the records of a business noticed that the address on an invoice from a cleaner had been spelt incorrectly. He also noticed that the name of the cleaner was rather unusual. So he went round to see the place. When he knocked on the door he was surprised to find himself being greeted by two elderly sisters who had lived at the property for over 60 years. They had never heard of the so-called 'cleaner'. The inspector's suspicions were further aroused when he realised that the cleaner's name, 'R. Shastay', was an anagram of the word 'ashtrays'.

Inspectors often come across unusual names among the employees listed on companies' payrolls. These range from D. Duck and M. Mouse to O. B. Laden and the unlikely Bert Einstein. Such fictitious characters are listed in order to pad out a company's expenses, reduce its profits and thereby reduce its tax.

It is never a good idea to try and destroy evidence. One dodgy finance director kept incriminating books and records in an outbuilding where he thought leaking rain would render them illegible. When his fraud was uncovered he set out to burn the books and destroy them once and for all. But he couldn't. They were too damp.

HMRC now has the same investigative powers as its more 'pro-active' colleagues in Customs & Excise. And these are considerable. It can in extreme cases bug phones and intercept e-mails and letters without any outside authorisation. One adviser says that these powers come as no surprise to him because he always knew there were 'a lot of buggers in HMRC'.

HMRC also has powers to demand that taxpayers hand over documents, and these powers have increased over the decades. The taxman can now obtain a warrant to search premises and seize documents, and the definition of what constitutes a document has been updated for the modern era. It is now considered to be 'anything in which information of any description is recorded'. That, HMRC has made clear, includes hard disks, floppy disks, CDs and any other electronic method of storage. It can even include information that is only recorded in the taxpayer's head.

Reasons for non-disclosure

Inspectors will accept a number of excuses for lost documents or for the late filing of tax returns. But 'the dog ate it' is not one of them...

The acceptable excuses include:

- Fire or flood in the post office where the documents were handled;
- Prolonged industrial action by Post Office staff;
- Loss through fire, flood or theft. (Note, though, that the top-floor offices of accountants are statistically as likely to be flooded as the higher slopes of Mount Ararat... and that putting a lit cigarette close to the only copy of last year's accounts does not count);
- Very severe illness, such as a coma, a serious heart attack, a stroke or any other life-threatening

condition – though here it is as well to note that the possibility of an HMRC enquiry is not (as yet) of itself considered to be a life-threatening condition;

- The death of a close relative or (domestic) partner 'shortly before the deadline'. This phrase is included for those who might be hoping that gran's sad demise a decade ago can be made to count.

There are a number of excuses that HMRC has made it clear it will not accept. At the top of this list stands 'shortage of funds'. Having no money is not considered a reasonable pretext for not paying tax. Moreover the old chestnut 'I won it at the dogs' is a gambit that rarely works. Casino records can be checked these days under money-laundering legislation, and inspectors know that any money that has been bet on the dogs is more likely to have gone to the dogs than anywhere else.

Other unacceptable excuses include:

- Claiming that the forms are too difficult to complete (though HMRC does sometimes seem to be pushing taxpayers to try this one in the courts);
- The pressure of work;
- The shortcomings of a financial intermediary/tax agent;
- A lack of information;

- The absence of reminders from HMRC;
- Being away on holiday.

And, by the way, in the world of Google maps and sat-nav systems, it is not acceptable to claim that you cannot find the office where the taxman scheduled your next meeting.

Another reality of today's world is that it is a global world. More and more UK taxpayers speak funny languages. But they should not imagine that they can hide behind them when they get onto HM's roller coaster. As their work has become more international, tax inspectors have learned more foreign languages. There are now Russian speakers and Mandarin speakers among them, and several understand different Indian dialects. So don't start talking to your tax adviser in a foreign tongue, telling them that you're never going to reveal where the money is even if someone pulls out your fingernails. Should no one employed by HMRC speak your particular version of Serbo-Croat, the taxman will not hesitate to call in interpreters.

Inspectors are also highly skilled at understanding unspoken languages – the way in which letters are constructed, for instance, and the body language of people attending meetings. It is no good insisting to your adviser that you are going to attend a meeting and promise that when you're there you 'won't say a word'. Because when you are there, you will. It is not possible to walk into a room without communicating something to whoever is present.

7

Other sources of information

It could all end in TIEAs

Stolen data is an increasingly valuable source of information for HMRC. Nowadays it can come from something as simple as a disgruntled employee downloading information onto a memory stick and forwarding it to the authorities. In July 2012, a wealthy UK property developer who had hidden money in a secret Swiss bank account was the first person to be convicted of tax evasion in a case involving stolen data.

Information gained via inter-governmental relationships is also now a key source. Anti-money-laundering and anti-terrorism laws have facilitated a far greater flow of information between countries. Ostensibly, such legislation is designed to help in the pursuit of international terrorists, arms dealers and drug traffickers by cutting them off from their sources of finance. And, since theirs are essentially cash businesses, the legislation has been aimed at preventing large cash transactions from passing through the financial system.

It goes without saying that few terrorists or drug dealers fill in their tax returns honestly, if they fill them in at all. Hence most money-laundering cases involve large amounts of unpaid tax, and the two activities – tax avoidance and money laundering – have become increasingly intertwined. It sometimes seems as if the authorities want to suggest that anyone avoiding tax must also be involved in money laundering.

There has also been a notable recent increase in bilateral Tax Information Exchange Agreements (TIEAs) following the G20's 'Global Forum on Tax Transparency' in 2009. The latest Swiss–UK tax agreement is a sort of super-TIEA. It forces Swiss banks to inform HMRC of the top ten destinations to which money removed from Switzerland has been sent. In addition, the European Savings Directive gives all EU tax authorities access to details of interest earned by residents from financial institutions in almost all other EU member states.

TIEAs are the 'new big thing' and countries have to have at least twelve in order not to be on the OECD's blacklist of fiscal ne'er-do-wells. The OECD is now coordinating efforts by the G20 to introduce standardised exchanges of information between member states. Its proposals include a definition of what financial information is to be exchanged automatically – a definition that includes data on interest, dividends, sales proceeds from financial assets, and other income generated by assets.

The OECD is also concerned to see that the right legal and administrative framework is in place for these automatic exchanges of information to function effectively. It wants to ensure confidentiality and avoid misuse of the data that is transmitted. That means putting checks on how widely the data is dispersed. In the UK the taxman is already allowed to share information with other government agencies, including the police, the Charity Commission and the Serious Fraud Office.

Elementary, my dear Batman

Despite all this, HMRC still depends heavily on good old-fashioned investigatory skills. These range from sophisticated data-mining to more surface-level observations. For example, it may spot your Porsche Cayenne and your new swimming pool even if they are not visible from the main road. (It has been known to use Google Earth and Street View to identify inconsistencies between residents' declared income and their lifestyle.)

The taxman also uses internet research and government databases to identify undeclared foreign property income and gains. (Most holiday rentals are advertised

on the internet.) And it's not only celebrities who boast on Twitter about their luxury homes and lifestyles. As part of a recent focus on e-commerce, HMRC used the internet to spot what it called 'anomalies', 'lifestyle indicators' and 'unexplained inconsistencies' that threw up discrepancies between reality and the information that had been provided in tax returns.

HMRC's structure is now such that it can collate data in a way that makes it focus its efforts on those taxpayers most likely to be infringing the law. Its so-called Affluent Unit and its HNWI Unit are among a number

of initiatives aimed both at providing better 'customer service' and at tackling tax evasion through offshore bank accounts and assets. The Affluent Unit was set up in September 2011 to deal with the 200,000-odd people who have a net worth of between £2.5 million and £20 million. The HNWI unit covers individuals with net worth of over £20 million.

There is also what is called an 'Offshore Co-ordination Unit' (OCU). This was set up to manage the information that HMRC regularly receives from different sources around the globe. The OCU's boss has claimed that the vast amount of data that it has to manage is '80 times more than the British Library'.

Codes of Practice

There are two types of major investigation undertaken by her majesty's inspectors. One is carried out under the rules of what is known as Code of Practice 8; the other under those of Code of Practice 9.

In cases brought under COP8 rules, there are generally large amounts of tax involved and complex arrangements. These include 'marketed' avoidance schemes that have often been sold with legal counsel's opinion that such arrangements are legitimate.

The 'Code of Practice 9' investigation process (now also known as the Contractual Disclosure Facility, or CDF) is followed whenever fraud is suspected. With COP9, HMRC expects to see the taxpayer face to face; there is no such expectation with COP8. And again with COP9, the taxpayer submits a formal report to HMRC outlining the fraud and the tax due. With COP8 there is no hard and fast requirement to produce such a report.

The COP9 process was changed dramatically in 2012. In general, HMRC now sends the taxpayer a letter saying that it suspects tax fraud (see page 17). The letter invites the taxpayer to disclose whatever he may have kept hidden. The taxpayer can deny tax fraud. Or he can accept the Revenue's invitation to enter into the CDF process. If the taxpayer accepts, then he has to admit to the relevant fraudulent activities and produce a written outline disclosure of them within 60 days. In those 60 days, HMRC will not liaise at all with the taxpayer or his advisers.

After the 60 days are up, if the taxpayer has made a disclosure, HMRC will check whether it accords with the information that it has gathered and then decide whether to accept the taxpayer into the CDF process. If he is accepted, HMRC agrees that it will not start a criminal investigation of the offences in question. Then the procedure more or less follows the lines of the previous Code of Practice 9, with one important difference. In any meeting under the old rules, taxpayers were asked a series of formal questions – five in cases of direct tax; four for indirect tax. Now there are no formal questions at all, just an awful lot of informal ones.

8

Professional advisers

The fount of (almost) all wisdom

Getting professional advice is a sure way to reduce the pain of an investigation. A cool and early analysis of the issues is the key to a successful conclusion. That is something you are unlikely to achieve with a man you sat next to on Disney's Big Thunder Mountain, nor with the mate whose flat you shared back in the eighties, whom everybody says is now a financial whiz living in Cloud Cuckoo Land.

A professional adviser can be a shoulder to cry on, a source of technical knowledge, and a fount of sound practical advice based on the fact that he or she has probably seen it (almost) all before. He or she might, for instance, suggest that a taxpayer visiting HMRC leave his Patek Philippe watch at home. Even watches designed by the Swiss to last for several generations may not withstand the gravity-defying pressure of HMRC's tighter twists.

It is also a good idea to flash one of London Underground's Oyster cards when enjoying the hospitality of HMRC. For the taxman is wary of expensive modes of transport. Private jets and super-yachts turn him green with suspicion, and that is not a pretty sight. He tends to believe that a corporate CEO's ego profits far more from such trinkets than do the businesses that he is supposed to run. And 'massaging one's ego' is not a deductible expense in the taxman's eyes.

Initially, advisers may seem expensive. But at the end

of the day they can save their clients a great deal of money – usually far more than their bills. In extreme cases, they even manage to keep their clients out of jail. Advisers who have been in the business for some time swear that had they been working on a contingency basis – whereby they earned a percentage of the tax that they saved – they would by now be very wealthy indeed.

One of the biggest benefits of having an adviser is the continuous communication that he or she has with HMRC. Advisers spend their lives dealing with tax inspectors. If anyone understands these strange creatures and their behaviour, they do. An adviser can phone an inspector if a deadline is approaching and fend off the risk of a heavy-handed reminder. It is a rare taxpayer who will feel sufficiently relaxed about his affairs to be able to do the same.

As far as HMRC is concerned, a taxpayer can choose to be represented professionally at any stage in the proceedings. Sometimes the first encounter with a roller coaster can be scarier than the visitor imagines. The need to have a friendly hand to hold suddenly becomes pressing. Taxpayers are free to change advisers in mid-stream (even in the middle of a water chute should they so wish). HMRC will deal with whatever is put before it.

Advisers often end up becoming their clients' confidants. In the circumstances they find themselves in, clients soon realise that there are few people they can fully trust with the details of their affairs. Moreover, advisers' offices are often situated in the centre of large cities. A visit there can be combined with a trip to an exhibition and a bit of serious shopping. The office can easily become a place of refuge, a place where the taxpayer lets off steam with tea and sympathy... and with a good packet of biscuits. Every adviser needs to serve good biscuits.

Some of what is disclosed to an adviser is covered by the law on privilege. But a recent Supreme Court case, Prudential v HMRC, confirmed that not all of it is. For example, a client who is seeking accountancy advice 'in contemplation of litigation' may claim privilege only for documents that have been created with the prospect of that litigation in mind. But it is always best to clarify with an adviser at the very beginning of the relationship what is and what is not covered by the law on privilege. And don't assume the law is the same as it was when you were last advised about it.

In any case, it is now mandatory for any professional-services firm in the UK (lawyers, accountants, bankers, brokers and so on) to produce what is known as a SAR (Suspicious Activity Report) whenever they suspect that one of their clients may have been up to no good. These reports are automatically made available to HMRC.

Strategic direction

Once a taxpayer has come under investigation, it is important for him (or her) to work out a strategy. This involves deciding what a reasonable settlement might be. The amount that is fixed upon might have to be modified as information becomes available during the process of the investigation, but it is as well to define an end right at the beginning. That makes it so much easier to attain that end… in the end.

In a lot of cases (yes, really, a lot) advisers can broadly

tell within the very first hour of the very first meeting how the case is going to progress. They cannot forecast the actual outcome, of course, but they do get to know the parameters. For one thing, attitude is important. It does not pay to be too casual and to act as if you don't know what all the fuss is about. Inspectors don't like it, for example, when they ask a taxpayer about his travels in a particular year and are told they were 'much the same as the year before'.

With bigger cases, it is more difficult to decide on a strategy. Yet a clear plan of how the process is to be managed is essential. This plan should be prepared with the taxpayer's advisers and, on occasions, with HMRC. Sharing problems (agoraphobia, claustrophobia, acrophobia, and so on) with the staff before a ride can sometimes be helpful.

In cases of suspected fraud, the Revenue first has to decide whether to pursue a criminal prosecution. (There were 617 prosecutions for evasion in 2012/13.) Those who are not going to be prosecuted will then be offered a chance to participate in the CDF process. At that point the taxpayer needs specialist advice, because he will be presented with a number of options. Choosing the wrong one can be like drawing a 'Go to Jail' card in Monopoly.

Throughout the process inspectors do try to be non-confrontational. But they hold their cards close to their chest. When they ask about the schooling of your

beloved offspring, they are not genuinely interested in little Crispin's educational prowess. All they want to know is, what fees are being paid, and how?

Although the taxpayer is under no legal obligation to say anything during the interviews, it is surprising how many of them end up chattering like magpies in a magic garden, desperately trying to find excuses for inexcusable behaviour. At such times it is best to observe the old adage, 'When in a hole, stop digging.' 'When in a magic garden, stop chattering.'

Anyone who comes under HMRC's beady eye for

allegedly unpaid taxes and, at the time, no longer lives within the UK's jurisdiction and has no assets whatsoever within the UK, faces a rather different type of decision-making and negotiation. Here the non-taxpayer can afford to say, 'Come and get me if you want me.' And anybody who is comfortably settled in the Ukraine or Somalia may find that this ploy works remarkably well. If, however, they should at some stage subsequently wish to return to the UK (be it even for a day) and not face the risk of incarceration, they will need to reach a settlement with the taxman first.

9

The investigation

Journey through Never Land

Tax investigations can sometimes sound like a Peter Pan fantasy, a sort of Journey through Never Land, the world created by J. M. Barrie where children never grow up. Taxpayers have been known to behave in remarkably childish ways in the presence of inspectors. They throw peevish fits sometimes, and have even been known to cry out for their mothers.

In west Wales, the Oakwood Theme Park's Journey to Neverland is described as being an 'interactive walk-through experience'. Much as taxpayers might wish it were so, the tax inspector's world cannot in all honesty be described as a walk-through experience. Nor is it inhabited by fairies. But, as in Never Land, not everything there is quite as it seems. The taxman's language, for instance, can often be confusing.

Take the word 'hypothetically'. When used by inspectors it tends to mean that whatever follows is actually not hypothetical at all; it is exactly what happened

– as in, 'Hypothetically you could have been putting it all into a bank account in the British Virgin Islands,' or 'Hypothetically you could have bought Disneyland with that much money.'

The following phrases – other recurring favourites of tax inspectors – are also less than totally transparent:

- 'Serious consequences', as in 'Serious consequences could follow from that.'
- 'We are disappointed in your report', meaning, 'We have found significant omissions in it.'
- 'Can I come and see you again sometime soon?' After an exhausting visit from the taxman it is tempting to say, 'No, I never want to see you again.' But that would be the wrong answer. Say 'Yes', unless you want the inspector to serve a notice which forces you to disclose documents that you might otherwise have been able to keep to yourself.

Taxpayers themselves sometimes use language that is as opaque as a tunnel in a haunted house. For example, they often start by saying, 'I want to meet these people. I want this sorted. And I want it sorted now.' But not only is such bullish talk not helpful, it is in almost all cases not true. Nobody really wants to meet tax inspectors. And certainly not 'Now'. In any case, there is rarely any need for a taxpayer to meet HMRC directly. Most of the contact is done by advisers. In CDF cases, a taxpayer and his tax inspector might meet on a couple of occasions at the beginning and the end of the process.

Other favourite sayings of distressed taxpayers include:

- 'Somebody told me this is what happened to him,' when what they really mean is, 'This is exactly what happened to me.'
- 'I don't care if this thing goes on for years,' which means something like, 'If we can't finish this by next weekend I'm going to have a heart attack.'
- 'I'm going to pay them £50,000 to get them off my back.' Note that £50,000 is the standard opening figure when a final settlement seems likely to be in the region of £1 million.

10

Legal procedures

Hocus Pocus Hall

HMRC has recently been trying to find ways to avoid expensive and time-consuming court appearances for intransigent cases. To that end it has introduced a number of alternatives to entering the halls of justice – the 'Hocus Pocus Halls' as many taxpayers feel inclined to call them once they have seen the wizardry that takes place there.

The most significant new process is the **Liechtenstein Disclosure Facility** (LDF). Introduced in 2009, this is an agreement with the Liechtenstein government giving UK taxpayers with assets in Liechtenstein a partial amnesty, low penalties and protection from prosecution if they come clean. (Some taxpayers without such assets have opened a Liechtenstein bank account in order to take advantage of HMRC's atypical generosity.) Similar facilities were set up subsequently with Jersey, Guernsey and the Isle of Man.

In 2011 HMRC came to a rather different agreement with Switzerland. The UK–Swiss Tax Cooperation

Agreement, which came into force in 2013, is neither an amnesty nor an opportunity to negotiate a deal. It gives Swiss bank account holders a chance to declare all their assets and pay the tax and penalties due, or not to declare them and then to have an arbitrary amount withheld from their assets in Switzerland. In practice this is a 'no brainer'. For there is a specific place in the taxpayer's future returns for the disclosure of these assets and accounts! As part of the deal, the Swiss government paid over £250 million to HMRC. Such a deal would have been inconceivable ten years ago.

From 2 September 2013, a new ride called the Alternative Dispute Resolution (ADR) was made available to taxpayers. This offers a short cut for SMEs (small and medium-size enterprises) and individuals to resolve tax disputes. ADR brings in an independent third party (called a 'mediator'), someone who has not previously been involved in the case. The mediator works with both the taxpayer and the tax inspector to try to broker an agreement between them. Entering into the ADR process does not affect a taxpayer's other rights of appeal.

Another relatively new feature is called 'the Employee Benefit Trusts (EBT) settlement opportunity'. This is a process operated by HMRC which allows taxpayers to conclude any dispute over their Employee Benefit Trusts without having to go to a tribunal (see page 81). Legislation introduced in March 2011 put beyond doubt that such schemes do not work. With the settlement opportunity, HMRC is inviting users of the schemes to pay up without recourse to litigation.

In addition, the introduction of a number of new units within HMRC has brought in specialist expertise more able to reach early settlements with taxpayers. In January 2013, the Affluent Compliance Team, a unit that focuses on taxpayers with an annual income of more than £150,000 and wealth of over £1 million, began to recruit 100 additional inspectors as the work of the unit expanded.

When cases do end up in court there is no doubt that the Revenue tends to win them, if only for the simple reason that it takes to court only those cases that it feels it is pretty sure to win. That said, however, it does not win them all (see pages 82–3).

The right to appeal

There is always a small percentage of people who feel disgruntled about their experience with HMRC. 'I'm going to complain about you to a higher authority' is their favourite line. For taxpayers who feel they have reasonable grounds for complaint, there is a standard procedure which allows them to appeal to more senior officials. And this is sufficient to sort out most cases.

For anyone who wants to take matters further, there is also an 'impartial referee' called the Revenue Adjudica-

tor, to whom complaints can be addressed. Anyone wishing to go beyond this has the right to ask their MP to refer their case to the independent parliamentary ombudsman.

Some taxpayers have been tempted to suggest that their human rights have been abused during the course of an investigation. And European human-rights legislation has been called upon occasionally in UK tax cases. But don't attempt to use these various complaints procedures for tactical purposes. Unless you feel you have really good cause to complain, they are not going to help.

Anyone who feels that a ruling by HMRC (as opposed to their treatment by HMRC) has not been fair also has a right to appeal. Before April 2009, such appeals were heard in another part of Hocus Pocus Hall by one of two different bodies, one called the General Commissioners, the other the Special Commissioners.

Since April 2009, however, appeals have been heard by a tribunal. And here Hocus Pocus Hall becomes even more labyrinthine. For there are two levels of tribunal: a so-called 'first tier' and an 'upper tier'. A first-tier tribunal is the first port of call. Its decisions bind the parties to the case and leave no right to any further appeal. If the case is a 'lead case' then it similarly binds those cases which follow behind it. However, a first-tier tribunal judgement does not create a legal precedent, whereas a judgement that comes from the upper tier does.

After an appeal to a tribunal, a taxpayer still has the right to appeal directly to the courts.

There have been occasional suggestions that taxpayers are not nowadays being treated as fairly as they used to be. Those who argue along these lines point to rules that were introduced in 2008 giving HMRC's investigators new powers to seek out information. They can now, for example, enter and inspect business premises in order to look into a specific individual's tax affairs. And nobody, either inside the business or outside it, has the right to appeal against their 'raid'. When the business

Honest, m'lud; it's only a stud

One of HMRC's most notorious court failures
established a principle that became known as the
Hastings-Bass rule (after Peter Hastings-Bass, a
racehorse trainer who died in 1964, and whose
granddaughter is the well-known sports
commentator Clare Balding). The case involved
giving relief for the adverse tax consequences of
mistakes made by trustees. The ruling in the
Hastings-Bass case allowed the courts to declare
void any such decision which had results other than
those originally intended

In a later case (the Futter case) the Supreme Court
ruled that the Hastings-Bass rule should apply only
where there had been a breach of fiduciary duty by
trustees. As there had been no such breach in
Futter's case (as the trustees had taken professional
advice which, unfortunately, proved to be incorrect),
no relief was available for the capital-gains tax
liability which had inadvertently arisen.

This settled some of the confusion and uncertainty
surrounding application of the Hastings-Bass rule.
It also considerably limited the circumstances in
which relief could be given by the courts.

The rules were changed again, however, by yet another case, called the Pitt case. Heard in the Supreme Court at the same time as the Futter trial, it reversed a Court of Appeal ruling that no relief was available for an individual who mistakenly believed that a transfer into a trust would not give rise to an inheritance-tax liability. The Supreme Court decided that the gravity of the mistake, and the consequences for the person who made the relevant transaction, must be taken into account. And it ruled that the test for granting relief had been satisfied.

Hastings-Bass lives on, at least in part, in Jersey, where legislation passed in 2013 effectively incorporated into law 'the rule in Hastings-Bass', a rule that had been established almost 50 years earlier.

premises are part of someone's home, however, the raiders can be kept out of the domestic part of the building.

Developments such as this nurtured demands for a formal Taxpayers' Charter setting out each taxpayer's basic rights and responsibilities (including a statutory

right to appeal). In April 2009, the government announced that a charter would be produced, and it can now be found on a government website. It includes lists of the taxpayer's rights and obligations (see box opposite).

Any such charter must have teeth, though, and this one has yet to prove that it has any. Without molars it is as useless as a notice at the entrance to Hocus Pocus Hall saying: 'Beware All Ye Who Enter Here'.

HMRC's 'Taxpayers' Charter'

What you can expect from us:

1 Respect you;
2 Help and support you to get things right;
3 Treat you as honest;
4 Treat you even-handedly;
5 Be professional and act with integrity;
6 Tackle people who deliberately break the rules and challenge those who bend the rules;
7 Protect your information and respect your privacy;
8 Accept that someone else can represent you; and
9 Do all we can to keep the cost of dealing with us as low as possible.

What we expect from you:

1 Be honest;
2 Respect our staff; and
3 Take care to get things right.

11

Compliance

The Petting Farm

A visit to HMRC is carefully scheduled, with the different 'attractions' being allocated specific times. For example, the Mae West letter (see page 17) has to be sent within 12 months of the due date of filing the tax return – normally by the end of January each year. So anyone who has not received a letter by 31 January 2015 concerning their tax liability for the year 2012/13 (for which the return was due by the end of January 2014) cannot be subject to a random enquiry.

However, don't imagine that failing to file a return in time lets you off the ride completely. Penalties are imposed when deadlines are not met (see box on pages 88–9). Also, HMRC can open an enquiry at any time during the subsequent 20 years should it come across hitherto undiscovered 'material' information or serious fraud. Failure to file a tax return, albeit careless rather than deliberate, is considered material.

HMRC's offices are scattered across the country.

There are three main centres – in Glasgow, Liverpool and Newcastle – which act as sorting offices from which correspondence and cases are redistributed. Newcastle handles all self-assessment cases.

There are no 'local' offices any more to which taxpayers can go and see the man who is in charge of their file. But there are some specialist units that deal with particular issues. The Birmingham-based Offshore Co-ordination Unit (OCU), for example, deals with most cases involving foreign income and capital. The Specialist Investigations (SI) unit – formerly known as the Special Civil Investigations (SCI) unit – is an elite squad of investigators who are rolled out to deal with serious cases wherever in the country they arise. They work on the side of the business that novelists and journalists are drawn to first.

Taxpayers should beware of having their photograph taken when paying a visit to the taxman's centres. There are plenty of cameras around ready to snap those memorable moments – the scream of horror, for instance, when you feel you are drowning in a river of detail. But don't be caught off guard. One taxpayer was filmed jumping for joy on the pavement outside an inspector's office just after a meeting.

HMRC has not yet fully embraced the internet and modern electronic technology. Its centres do not, for instance, include Angry Birds activity parks. Inspectors use

Significant deadlines

31 October – the date for submission of paper-based tax returns. Anything that arrives after this date gives rise to an automatic £100 penalty.

31 January – the deadline for submitting online tax returns. Again, any delay gives rise to a £100 fine.

31 January is also the last day for the payment of any tax still owing for the tax year that ended on the previous 5 April. Daily interest is charged on payments received after the due date. (Taxpayers may also be asked to make a 'first payment on account' for the current tax year.)

28 February – if tax that was due by 31 January is still unpaid by this date, then an automatic late-payment penalty of 5 per cent will be added to the amount still owing. (This is in addition to any interest payments that may be rolling over.)

31 July – for taxpayers who are making payments on account, this is the deadline for the second payment of tax owing for the previous fiscal year.

Also, at this point, anyone still owing tax that was due by the previous 31 January will be charged a second automatic 5 per cent late-payment penalty on top of the amount owed.

(In 2010/11 many new penalties for late filing and for late payment were introduced, but they are too numerous and complicated to be listed here.)

e-mail and other electronic communications sparingly, and online booking of appointments is not yet possible. When they do send e-mails, however, they tag on a return message which advises them when the original was opened. This eliminates opportunities for taxpayers to use 21st century versions of 'the dog ate it' – excuses like 'it was infected by a fatal virus'.

12

Debt enforcement

The Slammer

Many people who become subject to an HMRC investigation want to know, early on, how much it is going to cost them. Such people are often successful businessmen who have grown used to knowing the price of everything before they make a decision about anything. Does the entrance fee to the roller-coaster ride include the cost of a sick bag, for instance? And does my 17-year-old tattooed layabout count as a child when it comes to the special rates for kiddies?

There are three elements to the cost of a tax investigation.

* There is the amount of previously unpaid tax, which will have to be paid;
* There is the interest on that tax (which can be considerable if it has remained unpaid for a number of years); and
* There are a number of penalties that HMRC will

impose for any incorrect returns that they have been provided with. (Think of these as fines for lying.) The bigger the amount omitted from the return, the bigger the penalty.

Too many taxpayers become unhealthily obsessed with the third of these – the penalties that they might have to pay. But this is wrong-headed. The thing to focus on is mitigating the tax. At the end of the day, both the interest due and the penalty are determined by it.

The penalty is influenced by three factors: the amount of tax understated (i.e., the amount that was omitted from the taxpayer's returns); the taxpayer's behaviour in making the understatements; and the extent to which the taxpayer was helpful during the inspector's enquiry. In general, comments like 'I don't remember' and 'I don't care if this thing goes on for years' are not considered helpful.

Since 1 April 2009, the same regime of penalties has been applied across the whole range of taxes and duties. Before that there were different penalties for different taxes, which made the calculation about as straightforward as King Arthur's Labyrinth.

It is worth trying to keep the penalties as small as possible, because HMRC has some discretion in this area. For returns and documents submitted before 1 April 2009, fines could amount to 100 per cent of the tax due.

However, these can be mitigated by:

a) Up to 20 per cent for helpful disclosure;
b) An additional 10 per cent for voluntary disclosure;
c) Up to another 40 per cent for co-operation during the enquiry; and
d) Up to a further 40 per cent depending on the seriousness of the offence.

Technically this could amount to 110 per cent, but in practice HMRC limits it to 100 per cent.

For returns and documents relating to the period after April 2008 and submitted to HMRC on or after 1 April 2009, a completely new penalty regime applies. In cases of direct tax, HMRC differentiates between four different 'behaviours', as it calls them – innocent error, carelessness, deliberate offences, and deliberate offences that are concealed.

Innocent errors include instances, for example, where widows are tidying up their late husbands' affairs and they are genuinely not aware that the man's overseas foundations were largely cosmetic. But such cases are rarer than taxpayers would like to believe.

In an attempt to differentiate between the four types of behaviour, inspectors are beginning to ask taxpayers for their curriculum vitae in order to judge what constitutes carelessness in each individual case. It is different, for example, for someone with a law degree from someone who left school at 16.

It is as if Alton Towers were to compensate riders on the Smiler for their stomach-churning discomfort and then decide to base the level of compensation on the rider's educational standard. Anyone with three A levels should know full well what they are letting themselves in for… and therefore get nothing: 17-year-old layabouts, on the other hand, might be offered compensation when they throw up, on the grounds of their general ignorance.

Neither the unpaid tax, the interest on the tax, nor the penalties are going to be revealed with any degree of accuracy until somewhere near the end of the process, almost at the point when the taxpayer dismounts from the very last ride. The process is designed to motivate taxpayers to keep the investigation moving to an early conclusion.

At the end of the day the penalty can, in effect, become zero – in cases, for instance, where there is nothing more serious than an honest mistake. However, regardless of which regime applies (pre- or post-2008/2009), the unpaid tax and the appropriate interest on it are always due in full. For serious cases, the old and the new penalty rules may both apply until at least 2029. Which rules are applied to what will depend on the years involved.

Tax liabilities do not die immediately with us, although the European Court of Human Rights has said that tax penalties cannot be imposed on the living in respect of acts committed by a person or persons now deceased. HMRC has four years after someone's death in which to find out if there has been a problem with their returns, and then it can only reassess liabilities for the six tax years before the death. Only after that can the taxpayer truly RIP.

Walk-in possession

Inspectors have the right to seize an individual's 'moveable' assets in order to collect unpaid tax, and to do this they do not need to call on a bailiff. They just need to issue what is known as a 'walk-in possession order', and then they can come and take goods up to the value of the unpaid tax. They have also (since the 2014 Budget) been able to take money directly from a taxpayer's bank account. However, they cannot (yet) attempt to seize a taxpayer's home.

There are some other moveable assets that remain strictly out of bounds. These include the tools of a person's trade, the basic necessities of life, and perishable goods. Hence, since frozen food cannot be taken, neither can a freezer. To a taxpayer looking at his otherwise reduced circumstances, retaining a freezer might seem like cold comfort!

Jail is an unlikely final destination for riders on the taxman's roller coaster. But there is a trend today, when inspectors suspect taxpayers of other more serious criminal offences, of pursuing them with tax charges because they feel that gives them the best chance of putting the suspects behind bars. For obvious reasons, such cases have come to be known as 'Al Capone cases'.

Some tax offenders, however, are more likely than others to end up in prison: lawyers and accountants, for instance, (people who definitely should know better); repeat offenders; and people with words like Vanuatu or

Andorra on their letter heading. In one six-month period, HMRC issued only three press releases about prosecutions. They were headed, respectively:

- Tax credit cheat sentenced to community service;
- Unqualified accountant sentenced to 12 months for cheating;
- Tax cheat barrister loses appeal against jail sentence.

Although the tax barrister was convicted of cheating for his own account, rather than being involved in the cheating of his clients, it did not help his case (nor his sentencing – he got four and a half years) that he was a member of the bar. Sentences have been getting heavier in recent years, ever since a judge said in 2001 that the appropriate sentence for a large-scale effort to cheat HMRC should be between four and eight years in prison.

13

The VAT vampires

Unlucky for some

VAT vampires are to be found in many areas of HMRC. But they are particularly active around an amusement called the Carousel. This is a circular type of VAT fraud also known as MTic fraud. It features a budding criminal who buys up small high-value items in bulk from abroad – one particular case involved the purchase of mobile phones from Belgium. Lithuania is another popular starting point for this particular trick.

The criminal brings the goods quite openly into the UK, where they are zero-rated for VAT since they come from within the EU. (Both Belgium and Lithuania are full members.)

The importer then sells the goods within the UK to a number of different companies under his control in order to help disguise their origin. (This sale and resale of goods is the so-called 'Carousel'.) Having added VAT to his invoices, he then scarpers with the tax (to somewhere way beyond the borders even of Lithuania). The goods

are eventually sold by someone else (who may or may not be innocent of the scam) to the final consumer. Such scams have been known to involve unpaid taxes of as much as £100 million. One estimate suggests that HMRC lost over £1.3 billion from such schemes in a single year.

After a number of unsuccessful attempts to pursue the criminals involved in these scams directly, HMRC changed its tack. It began to deny the final vendors'

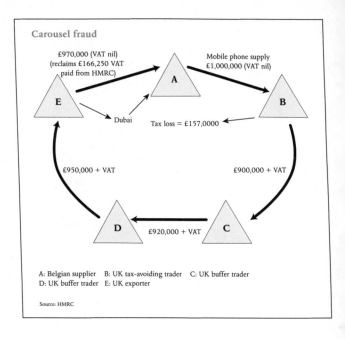

Carousel fraud

£970,000 (VAT nil)
(reclaims £166,250 VAT
paid from HMRC)

Mobile phone supply
£1,000,000 (VAT nil)

E → A → B

Dubai   Tax loss = £157,0000

£950,000 + VAT   £900,000 + VAT

D   £920,000 + VAT   C

A: Belgian supplier   B: UK tax-avoiding trader   C: UK buffer trader
D: UK buffer trader   E: UK exporter

Source: HMRC

claims for repayment of VAT on the goods, and it won about half the cases that it pursued. The tactic was unfair in that some of the final vendors to whom VAT repayments were denied had genuinely paid the tax. But the taxman argued that his first responsibility is to protect revenue. The pursuit of criminals comes second, and is primarily the responsibility of others.

Another area where fraud is rife is the taxation of carbon credits. Some of these (compliance market credits,

for example) are liable to VAT, while others (like verified emission reductions) are not. Falsely categorising a particular credit can result in considerable tax evasion.

Fags, booze and trawlers

Because Britain's tax regime for booze and fags is more onerous than that of its fellow members of the EU, there is no shortage of people prepared to risk bringing bottles and cartons into the country, by boat, train and plane, without paying UK tax. The rule is that people can bring in alcohol and tobacco duty free if it is for their own consumption – i.e., not for onward sale. But there are plenty of stories of huge warehouses in Calais where booze and fags are stored in massive quantities ready to be slipped across the Channel. More than a decade ago such smuggling was said to be costing HMRC almost £4 billion a year. There is no evidence to suggest that the amount has since declined.

Some of the UK's borders are more porous than others – that between Northern Ireland and the Irish Republic, for example, where differential prices on diesel fuel provide ample opportunities for smuggling and VAT evasion. And some of the means of transport used for smuggling are unconventional. North Sea trawlers, for example, have attracted the taxman's attention in the past – for their potential both to understate the value of their trawl and to carry cargoes other than fish.

14

Charities and trusts

Sharkbait Reef

Had she lived two centuries later than she did, Jane Austen might have slightly changed the opening sentence of *Pride and Prejudice*. 'It is a truth universally acknowledged,' she might have written, 'that a single man (or woman) in possession of a good fortune must be in want of a trust.'

For years, trusts have been used as a means to shelter income and capital gains from tax. There are a number of different types of trust – for example, discretionary, interest-in-possession, bare and nominee – all with their own tax rules. Charitable trusts in particular are being used increasingly as vehicles for tax evasion. Money allegedly collected to buy sunhats for occasional visitors to the Fairy Kingdom has, on occasions, been used to buy sunny flats for occasional visitors to the chairman's bedroom.

Between them, trusts and charities have much the same effect on tax inspectors as the word 'offshore'. They make him get out his binoculars and take a closer look. And what he invariably sees is some rough and rocky terrain, not dissimilar to offshore coral, an area where the unsuspecting can easily be misled and end up a bit like sharkbait on a reef.

Within HMRC there is a special department which deals with these and a number of other specialist aspects of personal tax. These include:

- Inheritance tax;
- Pension schemes;

- Employee shares and securities;
- Share assets valuation; and
- Capital gains.

The whole area of capital gains is a particularly rough and rocky one for the unwary. Whereas a taxpayer's income is relatively smooth, year on year, capital gains usually come in big one-off dollops, and these tend to flash warning signals. It is always wise for taxpayers who are about to realise a large capital gain to seek professional advice.

Anyone who puts property into a UK trust has an obligation to notify HMRC of the creation of such a trust. UK trusts that owe tax on income or gains have a responsibility to inform HMRC of the fact. Trustees need to file a self-assessment tax return to report such income or gains.

Foreign trusts – those where some or all of the trustees are not resident in the UK – are not created or administered under UK law. But they may trigger a tax charge under complex anti-avoidance rules, and HMRC will then want to be notified and paid accordingly. UK beneficiaries of foreign trusts need to be especially careful and should seek expert advice.

The taxman is particularly allergic to things like the GmbH (roughly equivalent to the English 'company with limited liability') and *stiftungs* and *anstalts*, rare

Some valid reasons for setting up a trust

- To look after assets for minors and to provide income for their education and welfare.
- To protect assets in certain special circumstances – for example, a potential divorce.
- To enable one beneficiary to enjoy income, but for the underlying capital to be retained for others.
- To make arrangements for the members of your family, including future additions.
- To help with tax planning – for example a 'will trust' can reduce inheritance-tax liability.
- For making gifts – because you can specify in what circumstances beneficiaries will receive those gifts.
- To protect assets when you do not want the beneficiary to have full control over them.
- For social reasons (e.g. to have something to brag about at the golf club).

specimens in the trust world believed to survive these days only in the remoter *schlosser* of Liechtenstein. They are a mix between a company and a trust, and their main advantage is that they make it very difficult for outsiders to find out who are the beneficiaries of the assets that they hold. An *anstalt* has no members, no participants and no shareholders. These exotic creatures are high on the list of endangered fiscal species.

15

The taxpayer

Visitor to the Forbidden Kingdom

Taxpayers come in all shapes and sizes. Some are petrified by the prospect of any sort of trip on the taxman's roller coaster, while others become agitated and aggressive as they approach the experience, long before they know what they are in for.

When they are nervous, people tend to talk too much. On a theme park's scarier rides they will turn to total strangers and tell them their whole life's story. But beware if any of your story involves the non-payment of tax. Your fellow rider may be just as scared as you. But he may also be a tax inspector, and however scared he is he will not forget the relevant details of your life. Your only hope then is that he gets flung out at the thirteenth loop.

Whatever a taxpayer's attitude to an investigation into his affairs, it is essential that he remain fit for its duration. He should take regular physical exercise, and if he does fall ill he should get a doctor's certificate to that effect. HMRC is not unsympathetic to ill health.

Taxpayers also need to be in the right frame of mind for an investigation. It is not generally helpful to be aggressive and in denial. They need to be realistic and polite. And they need to be punctual.

It is no good thinking of an investigation as yet another competition where the aim is to get away with paying the absolute minimum. The whole purpose of the process is to end up with a settlement, and without any criminal investigation.

Elderly concentration

For the most part, the taxman is indiscriminate in his choice of subjects for his attention. But occasionally he decides to look closely at one particular group of people. In recent years, for example, HMRC has targeted over 30 different industry groups, including London lawyers, on-line traders and construction workers.

Inevitably, an increasing number of people who come under investigation by the taxman are ill equipped, either mentally or physically, to cope with the experience. Societies throughout the developed world are ageing, and more and more wealth is accumulating in the hands of the elderly.

A taxpayer who is frail and elderly will not be subjected to interrogation, any more than he will be forced onto something called Oblivion or Submission when on a casual visit to see the flamingos. There is no need to flap. That does not mean, however, that there will be no investigation into his affairs.

Other groups in today's society are almost equally ill equipped for the taxman's scrutiny. The group known as BOBOs ('the Burnt Out But Opulent'), for example; people who work every minute that the clock registers. Technology has intensified the pace of their lives so much that BOBOs are hard pressed to find either the time or the energy demanded by a full investigation.

Likewise, self-made successful entrepreneurs find

visits to HMRC peculiarly demanding. In their worlds they are used to getting what they want, when they want it, and they have spent much of their lives trying to find ways round obstacles. The taxman's demand that they stop for a minute's Submission is just another obstacle that they need to find a way round.

For all of these groups there is also the shame and embarrassment of an HMRC investigation. It is not a natural subject of polite dinner-party conversation. ('Oh, please do tell me more. So after you'd hit him on the jaw and failed to get on to the Heathrow Express, what happened next?') Everyone has skeletons in their cupboards that they choose to keep hidden. Once they are caught up in a tax investigation, however, taxpayers may find they have to reveal some of those skeletons, and some of their innermost thoughts too. And not just to a professional adviser, but also to a government agency.

Family matters

Tax investigations can last for 12 months and more, especially if (as is often the case) they involve overseas assets. It can take ages, for instance, to get overseas banks to certify dividend or interest payments.

Long-drawn-out cases put tremendous pressure on relationships. It's a bit like queuing for hours for the Dragon's Fury with your wife, her sister and five children under the age of 10, none of whom are yours. Even with the best will in the world, family members will not see the situation in the same light as the person under investigation.

It is not entirely unknown for family members to see benefits for themselves in a taxpayer's distress. For example, an opportunity to establish rights over hitherto hidden assets may suddenly dawn on a partner who has for some time been eager to assert greater independence.

And as for children: well, the possibilities with them are countless. For a start, they have their inheritance to think of. And there may be a matter of trust funds which they fear are coming under threat. So it really is best not to involve them. They never did understand you, and they are not going to start doing so now. Finally, remember that the chances of your mother-in-law being on your side are not high.

Taxpayers also need to think carefully about the friends that they might want to take along with them to see HMRC. This is not the sort of trip that it is wise to chat about over a beer in the pub or at the golf club. The more we offload our woes to others, the more those others in turn need to offload to someone else. Before you know where you are the whole town is familiar with your case. Or, more likely, a grossly exaggerated version of your case in which thousands have become millions and 'a croft in the blooming highlands' has become 'a loft in the Virgin Islands'.

In most towns, it is worth remembering, there is at least one resident who is a tax inspector. For anyone under investigation, it is best to stick with 70-year-old advice from the Second World War: 'Careless Talk Costs Lives' and 'Silence Means Security'.

The worst sort of friend these days is a reporter. And that includes almost anyone who writes a blog or broadcasts information on internet services such as Facebook, YouTube or Instagram. Tax inspectors are as busy socially networking as the rest of us, and they too can Google stuff.

The end of the ride

The most common way for an investigation to end is by the issuance of a closure notice, a standard letter from HMRC declaring that it has closed an enquiry for good. After this a taxpayer cannot be quizzed about the same things again in respect of the same periods. A COP9 inquiry, however, can end with a contractual settlement. And, of course, death is another option.

But don't hope that by spinning out a case you can increase your chances of forgiveness. The Offshore Disclosure Facility (ODF) of 2007, heralded by some as an amnesty, was in fact no such thing. Taxpayers still had to come up with any unpaid tax that was due, plus the interest on it. The carrot was a reduction in the penalty to 10 per cent of the unpaid tax for those declaring income under the terms of the facility.

HMRC says that '50,000 taxpayers have come forward through the offshore disclosure facilities, generating £1 billion in tax, penalties and interest.' From the Revenue's point of view the facilities have been disappointing in that they have failed to flush out a high-profile case that could have acted as a further deterrent by showing how effective they had been.

There is nothing that HMRC likes better than the publicity surrounding a famous person who gets caught up in a tax investigation. In the case of the Queen's favourite jockey, Lester Piggott, his fame was matched by his foolishness. When he reached a (not insubstantial) settlement with HMRC for not paying his taxes he sent a cheque drawn on an account that had never been mentioned before. After that he ended up in prison and lost his chances of a knighthood.

A subsequent offer from the Revenue for voluntary disclosure, announced in the 2009 budget, did not give as generous a reduction in the penalty as had the first one. The government hoped to signal to taxpayers that they should not hold out for the next deal in the hope that the penalty would then be even lower.

Most people who have been subjected to an investigation find that all their aches, pains and illnesses disappear, on average, within 30 seconds of leaving Her Majesty's Roller Coaster. Experience has shown that the termination has a beneficial effect on several important aspects of life, including:

- Sleep;
- Sex;
- Digestion;
- Life expectancy; and
- The attitude of bank managers.

But don't think that your slate is clean as soon as you pass out of the fiscal theme park's gates. Those whose behaviour is considered to have been deliberate, and whose

liabilities exceed a certain level, can find themselves being 'named and shamed' on HMRC's website. Their names and addresses will be posted there for all the world to see (and that includes inquisitive journalists). Tax inspectors pursue cases to the bitter end, and nobody's slate is assuredly spotless until at least 20 years have passed. Moreover, if payments under the terms of a settlement are not made on time, the taxpayer very swiftly gets a call from

HMRC's debt-management team. And its calls have been known to continue way beyond the grave.

Appendix A

Our top ten tips

1. Keep calm and don't panic
An investigation often provokes a number of violent
emotions in those under scrutiny – not least sheer terror
at the thought of ending up in jail. In reality, very few
cases end in a custodial sentence. Don't assume the worst.

2. Get expert advice at the outset
If you are being investigated by HMRC, seek out independent financial advice from a reputable adviser who
specialises (and is experienced) in the field. You will need
somebody on your side who knows how HMRC oper-
ates and who can take some of the emotional strain off
your shoulders. It's also likely to be cheaper in the long
run.

3. Don't discuss your tax affairs with anyone but a small circle of tax advisers
Tempting though it might be to offload your woes at the
pub or the golf club, it's never a good idea – unless you

want the whole town to know the details of your case; and that might include a taxman. It's also almost certain that your friends' advice will be wrong and detrimental to your chances of reaching a settlement.

4. Don't lie to HMRC

The poet Sir Walter Scott once observed: 'Oh what a tangled web we weave, when first we practise to deceive.' It has become one of HMRC's favourite quotations. Tax inspectors have a particular aversion to lies, and even the most innocent ones can rebound in unexpected ways. So remember, the five simple rules to follow if you want to be sure to avoid a jail sentence:

- Don't lie to HMRC.
- Don't lie to HMRC.
- Don't lie to HMRC.
- Don't lie to HMRC.
- Don't lie to HMRC.

5. Don't assume HMRC is ignorant of anything

An HMRC investigator has a huge number of resources at his disposal and is not afraid to ask questions. Letting a former flatmate know that you paid for your house in the Dordogne in cash may cost you the chance of getting a good deal with the taxman should he begin investigating your affairs.

6. Be well prepared for meetings

No one prepares to fail; they fail to prepare. It is pointless trying to evade HMRC's questions with insufficient preparation – the investigator will simply use his statutory powers to force you to answer his questions. Your lack of preparation will then be deemed to be 'lack of co-operation'.

7. Make significant (but relevant) payments on account

HMRC sees this as an important sign of willingness to co-operate. It may also save you a large amount in interest, which accrues from the date when the tax should have been paid through to the day it is actually paid. On the other hand, overpayment of outstanding liabilities may lead HMRC to an unrealistic expectation of how much you owe. There is a fine balance here.

8. Don't try to destroy evidence

It's often unhelpful. If you don't have the appropriate records, HMRC may assume that you are trying to hide something even when in fact you are not. The onus of proof is usually on the taxpayer. By the way, the worst thing about fires is the water damage afterwards!

9. Never make a partial disclosure

Do not suffer from selective amnesia when disclosing

information – this is particularly distasteful to HMRC and is likely to lead to a more punitive settlement. HMRC takes into account lack of co-operation when determining the penalty to be paid as part of a settlement.

10. Once you have reached a settlement, don't offend again

HMRC takes a dim view of repeat offenders.

Appendix B

Some of our favourite excuses offered by taxpayers to HMRC

'God asked me to transfer the shares to my husband.'

'After seeing a volcanic eruption on the news I couldn't concentrate on anything.'

'I've been far too busy touring the country with my one-man play.'

'I met this chap on a plane and he said it was alright… [long pause] …he's dead now.'

'My bad back means I can't go upstairs.'

'I've been cruising round the world in my yacht and only picking up post when I'm on dry land.'

Whatever excuses you do dream up, you can be fairly sure that HMRC has heard them before.